CONTENTS

WE'RE A FAMILY

Many times, there's a certain picture people have in their heads of a **traditional** family: a father, a mother, and their kid or kids. However, all families are different. Sometimes, family members have special needs or **challenges**. Sometimes you can see these differences, but sometimes you can't. Families with special needs are still families!

Maybe you're part of a family with special needs. Maybe you have a friend who is. The important thing to remember is that we're all more alike than different.

Families with special needs come in many combinations. Some can have just a mom or dad. Some have two moms or dads. They're all families.

DIFFERENT DIFFERENCES

You might be the person in your family with special needs. You might have trouble learning or understanding some things. You might have trouble hearing or seeing. You might have a sickness you need to deal with. You might have to use a wheelchair or other tools to get around.

Or, the person with special needs might be one of your brothers or sisters. It might be one of your parents. There might be more than one person in your family with special needs.

Families with special needs come in all shapes and sizes. Some are small. Some are bigger!

Sometimes people with special needs have physical, or body-related, differences. They have trouble physically doing things or need more time to do them. Sometimes they can't see or hear quite the same. Sometimes they have a sickness and need medical care.

Sometimes special needs are **developmental** differences, such as autism. People with development differences often have trouble learning things or dealing with others. People can also have **behavioral** or **emotional** differences or issues. Sometimes, more than one of these things will go together.

Autism is a difference in how a person's brain develops. Someone with autism may have trouble doing certain things or behave in a different way.

LIFE ON WHEELS

Sometimes, physical differences mean that people might need special tools to help them do things or get around. Many people who can't walk or have trouble walking use a wheelchair.

If you or someone in your family uses a wheelchair, you might have to rearrange your home and yard to **accommodate** it. You may need to pay extra attention to your path when you're going for a walk or ride through your neighborhood. Remember that there's nothing wrong with using a wheelchair. It's a useful tool!

All people are different. Some people need glasses to help them see. Some people need wheelchairs to help them get around. It's great to have tools that can help us!

TIME AND ATTENTION

One main difference about families with special needs is that they may sometimes need to spend more time or attention on the member or members with those needs.

If your brother has trouble learning, your parents may have to spend more time helping him with schoolwork. They may have to help him with basic needs like washing up and getting dressed too, even if he's older than you. Sometimes you might feel a little **ignored** when this is the case.

Just remember that your parents love you too. In a family dealing with special needs, everyone must adapt, or change a little to deal with things.

OTHER CHALLENGES

Sometimes, siblings, or brothers or sisters, of family members with special needs feel like they need to be perfect all the time. Sometimes this is because they don't want their parents to have more to deal with. Sometimes they feel like they can never **complain** or that their problems are ignored. They feel like they always have to help and grow up fast.

If you feel this way, it's important to talk to someone. Tell your parents or another trusted adult about your feelings.

Even when you love your family member with special needs, it can be hard to deal with the difference in your family. Don't feel bad.

STRONGER TOGETHER

People who grow up in a home with a family member with special needs often have their own strengths too. They learn to be more **patient** and kinder to those with differences. They're more **empathetic**. They often learn to do things for themselves earlier in life.

Many times, families with a member with special needs grow stronger together. They become resilient, or able to bounce back after trouble. They learn to work together. They learn to focus on, or give attention to, their strengths.

It's not always easy, but people in families with special needs work—and play—together!

QUESTIONS AND ANSWERS

If you have a family member with special needs—or if you have special needs—you might get a lot of questions from your friends. They might want to know more about how your family is different. They might want to know about you or your family member's daily life.

Be honest. Tell them about how things are different but also how things are the same. If they say mean things, try not to be angry. Tell them that it's not OK to say such things.

Sometimes others might try to bully you if you or your family are different. Tell someone if this happens.

THE WRONG IDEA

Sometimes people can have misconceptions, or false ideas, about disabilities and special needs. They might think all people with physical differences aren't as smart. They might think that all people with some learning differences will never learn things, even if the truth is that it will just take more time.

If you hear these misconceptions from your friends, it's OK to correct them. Explain that everyone's different, and that's OK! One person with special needs isn't always just like someone else with special needs.

All people with special needs are different, and all families with special needs are different too.

WE'RE ALL SPECIAL

The words "special needs" can mean many different things. Families that have a member or members with special needs have differences, but they have many things that are just like other families too. They have challenges and problems. They have fun and laugh together. They deal with school and work and everyday life.

If you're a member of a family with special needs, remember that your family might be different, but it's still great. It's unique, or one of a kind. All families are!

GLOSSARY

accommodate: To make room for someone.

behavioral: Having to do with behavior, or the way a person acts.

challenge: Something that is hard to do.

complain: To express unhappiness.

developmental: Having to do with development, or the act of growing and changing.

emotional: Having to do with emotions, or feelings.

empathetic: Showing empathy, or the ability to share someone else's feelings.

ignore: To pay no attention to.

patient: Able to remain calm when waiting for a long time or dealing with problems.

traditional: Following what's been done for a long time.

INDEX

WEBSITES

Due to the changing nature of Internet links, PowerKids Press has developed an online list of websites related to the subject of this book. This site is updated regularly. Please use this link to access the list: www.powerkidslinks.com/akof/specialneeds

Published in 2021 by The Rosen Publishing Group, Inc.
29 East 21st Street, New York, NY 10010

Copyright © 2021 by The Rosen Publishing Group, Inc.

All rights reserved. No part of this book may be reproduced in any form without permission in writing from the publisher, except by a reviewer.

First Edition

Editor: Michelle Denton
Book Design: Reann Nye

Photo Credits: Cover kali9/E+/Getty Images Plus/Getty Images; Series Art Vladislav Noseek/Shutterstock.com; p. 5 nd3000/Shutterstock.com; p. 7 Jaren Jai Wicklund/Shutterstock.com; p. 9 SolStock/E+/Getty Images; p. 11 JohnnyGreig/E+/Getty Images; p. 13 LightField Studios/Shutterstock.com; p. 15 Maskot/Getty Images; p. 17 fatihhoca/E+/Getty Images; p. 19 imtmphoto/Shutterstock.com; p. 21 Huntstock/Brand X Pictures/Getty Images.

Library of Congress Cataloging-in-Publication Data

Names: Keppeler, Jill, author.
Title: Families with special needs / Jill Keppeler.
Description: New York : PowerKids Press, [2021] | Series: All kinds of families | Includes index.
Identifiers: LCCN 2020001358 | ISBN 9781725317819 (paperback) | ISBN 9781725317833 (library binding) | ISBN 9781725317826 (6 pack)
Subjects: LCSH: People with disabilities–Juvenile literature. | People with disabilities–Family relationships–Juvenile literature.
Classification: LCC HV1568 .K47 2021 | DDC 362.4–dc23
LC record available at https://lccn.loc.gov/2020001358

Manufactured in the United States of America

Some of the images in this book illustrate individuals who are models. The depictions do not imply actual situations or events.

CPSIA Compliance Information: Batch #CSPK20. For Further Information contact Rosen Publishing, New York, New York at 1-800-237-9932.

I0813305

ALL KINDS OF FAMILIES

FAMILIES WITH SPECIAL NEEDS

JILL KEPPELER

PowerKiDS press
New York